CHILDREN
OF THE GREAT
DEPRESSION

CHILDREN
OF THE GREAT
DEPRESSION

RUSSELL FREEDMAN

CLARION BOOKS ▪ NEW YORK

Clarion Books
a Houghton Mifflin Company imprint
215 Park Avenue South, New York, NY 10003
Copyright © 2005 by Russell Freedman

The text was set in 13-point Sabon.
Book design by Trish Parcell Watts.

www.houghtonmifflinbooks.com

Manufactured in China.

Library of Congress Cataloging-in-Publication Data

Freedman, Russell.
Children of the Great Depression / by Russell Freedman.
p. cm.
Includes bibliographical references and index.
ISBN 0-618-44630-3
1. Children—United States—Social conditions—20th century—Juvenile literature. 2. Children—United States—History—20th century—Juvenile literature. 3. Depressions—1929—United States—Juvenile literature.
4. United States—Social conditions—1933–1945—Juvenile literature.
I. Title

HQ792.USF738 2005
305.23'0973'0904—dc22   2005006506

ISBN-13: 978-0-618-44630-8
ISBN-10: 0-618-44630-3

SCP 10 9 8 7 6 5 4 3 2 1

FRONTISPIECE: A Young Hooverville resident, Circleville, Ohio.
Photo by Ben Shahn, summer 1938.

FOR ROSE,
WHO REMEMBERS IT WELL

CONTENTS

PICTURING THE GREAT DEPRESSION

Most of the pictures in this book were created by a dedicated band of federal photographers who fanned out across America during the 1930s and tried to capture with their cameras the heartbreak and hope of the national crisis known as the Great Depression. What they saw then through the camera's eye is, to a remarkable degree, what we remember about the Great Depression today.

Among them were some of the nation's most accomplished photographers, men and women such as Dorothea Lange, Walker Evans, Marion Post Wolcott, Carl Mydans, Russell Lee, Arthur Rothstein, and Ben Shahn, noted also as a painter and graphic artist. They were employed by the Farm Security Administration (FSA), one of the government programs introduced by President Franklin D. Roosevelt and his advisers to combat the

Depression. Armed with recently developed compact cameras like the 35mm Leica I and the twin-lens-reflex Rolleiflex, they wandered the United States, documenting the stark reality of the Depression and the accomplishments of federal aid programs.

Between 1935 and 1943, FSA photographers produced more than a quarter of a million images of American rural and urban life—one of the most ambitious attempts ever made to portray a society in photographs. Most of those images, meticulously catalogued and lovingly preserved, now reside in the Prints and Photographs Division of the Library of Congress. A large number are available for online viewing.

The FSA photographs convey in human terms the true meaning of economic statistics. So graphic are they, so vivid the people and circumstances they portray, that they offer us an immediate emotional connection with these people and their experience. They tell us something that words alone cannot express. They have become an inseparable part of our national memory, our common knowledge of an era that tested the American dream.

CHILDREN
OF THE **GREAT**
DEPRESSION

"THE SIGHT OF MY FATHER CRYING"

The cold reality of America's Great Depression was brought home to one twelve-year-old boy in 1931 when he came upon his father in the empty coal bin of the family's Brookline, Massachusetts, house. Many homes at that time were heated by coal rather than oil, gas, or electricity.

"We had owned a small bakery that had failed a few months before," the boy recalled. "A little later we lost most of our savings at a local bank that went under. We still had our house, and we were eating, which was more than could be said for some of our friends. But that was about all, and I guess the thought that he wouldn't be able to buy enough coal to get us through the winter was just too much for my father to take. . . . Things

Hanging out in front of a Dover, Delaware, drugstore.

Photo by John Vachon, July 1938

would get worse for us later on, and for a couple of years we were in really bad shape, but for me the low point of the depression will always be the sight of my father that day, crying in the coal bin."

In an era when a father's pride and self-respect depended on his traditional role as the family's breadwinner, the nation's economic crisis could bring the strongest man to his knees in tears. Most kids understood this. They realized that their families' troubles had been brought about by the Great Depression, not by some failing on the part of their father or mother. They could see how anguished their parents were, how heartbroken they felt when they could not provide for their family's needs.

Kids whose parents couldn't pay the grocer or the landlord, and who weren't old enough themselves to contribute to the family income, were often overcome by feelings of powerlessness and regret. "My mother cries because maybe we'll lose the store," a nine-year-old wrote to First Lady Eleanor Roosevelt. "I['m] always sorry, because I'm still very young and can't help out."

Hard times had come to America. During the Great Depression of the 1930s, millions of families were struggling to live on incomes so meager that the threat of disaster hung over them day after day. More than half the nation's children were growing up in families that did not have enough money to provide adequate food, shelter, clothing, or medical care. Some people were so poor, they went hungry. Children fainted in school because they had not eaten at home.

At soup kitchens run by private or municipal charities, desperate people waited for a free meal in lines that stretched for blocks. "We saw the city at its worst," wrote a Chicago social worker. "We saw . . . our friends, sensible and thrifty families, reduced to poverty. . . . One vivid, gruesome moment of those dark days that we shall never forget. We saw a crowd of some fifty men fighting over a barrel of garbage that had been set outside the back door of a restaurant. American citizens fighting for scraps of food like animals!"

People asked themselves, How could this happen in America? How long will this awful depression last? What does it mean for the future of our children?

The Great Depression had been triggered by the collapse of the New York stock market in October 1929. All through the 1920s, the nation's economy had been growing at a furious pace. Businesses were booming. Profits were higher than ever. Hoping to get rich quickly, people from all walks of life were buying stocks—shares of ownership in American industry. The New York Stock Exchange on Wall Street was the leading market for the buying and selling of stocks.

Investors called it the "Big Bull Market," and it seemed to many that the good times would never end. Stock prices went up and up and up, until those prices were much greater than many companies were worth. That's when the stock market started to act strangely. Prices dipped suddenly, only to zoom up again on an economic roller coaster ride.

On Thursday, October 24, 1929, stock prices took an alarming nose-dive. That was a sign of trouble ahead. Five days later—Tuesday, October 29, a date remembered today as "Black Tuesday"—the stock market suddenly failed, or "crashed," as prices tumbled in a dizzy free fall.

Investors panicked and rushed to sell their stocks before prices fell even further. But now, no one wanted to buy. In one disastrous day, billions of dollars' worth of stocks were wiped out. Stocks that had once sold for forty-eight or fifty dollars per share were now being offered for a dollar or less.

Jobless men wait for a free meal outside a New York City municipal lodging house during the harsh winter of 1932–33.

People who had bought shares of stock on credit, by borrowing money from banks, found themselves over their heads in debt.

What ignited the panic on Wall Street and the terrible depression that followed? Economists point to several causes, some of them quite complicated. One big problem was that millions of working people and small farmers did not earn enough money during the 1920s to buy all the automobiles, refrigerators, washing machines, and other goods pouring out of America's factories. For a while, people bought what they needed or wanted on the installment plan, on easy credit. But as debts mounted, they bought less and less.

Unsold goods piled up. As a result, businesses began to pull back, and factories slowed down production. That's when the economy faltered and stock prices plunged. "Did the thought ever enter our bone heads," asked humorist Will Rogers, "that the time might come when nobody would want all these things we were making?"

When the stock market crashed, confidence in the nation's economy seemed to be buried in the rubble. Investors were afraid to risk any more money. Consumers stopped spending. Factories shut down. Shops failed. Business came almost to a standstill.

At first, it seemed like just another depression, part of the natural economic cycle, something that happens every so often. The United States had already experienced at least seventeen economic downturns during its 150-year history, some more severe than others. But this one turned out to be horribly different. It came on faster, affected a larger part of the population,

Unemployed youth, Washington, D.C.
PHOTO BY JOHN VACHON, AUGUST 1938

and caused far more damage and suffering than any depression before it. It became known as the *Great* Depression because it was the greatest economic calamity the United States has ever known.

"I knew the Depression had really hit when the electric lights went out," recalled Robin Langston, who was growing up in Hot Springs, Arkansas. "My parents could no longer pay the $1 electric bill. The kerosene lamps went up in [our] home."

DEPRESSION SHOPPING LIST	
Corn flakes (8 oz. package)	$ .08
Milk (per quart)	.10
Gasoline (per gallon)	.18
Large toothpaste	.25
Leather basketball	1.00
Baseball glove and ball	1.25
Women's leather shoes	1.79
Kodak box camera	2.50
Men's leather shoes	3.85
Tricycle	3.98
Women's cloth coat	6.98
Men's wool suit	10.50
Two-wheel bicycle	10.95
Vacuum cleaner	18.75
Typewriter	19.75
Gas stove	23.95
Electric washing machine	47.95
Living-room radio	49.95
Used 1929 Ford	57.50
New Pontiac coupe	585.00

AVERAGE ANNUAL EARNINGS DURING THE DEPRESSION	
Hired farm hand	$ 216.00
Live-in maid	260.00
Steelworker	422.00
Waitress	580.00
Coal miner	723.00
Construction worker	907.00
Secretary	1,040.00
Public-school teacher	1,227.00
Civil-service employee	1,284.00
Airline stewardess	1,500.00
Engineer	2,520.00
College teacher	3,111.00
Doctor	3,382.00
Airline pilot	8,000.00

Grocery store on the South Side of Chicago.

PHOTO BY RUSSELL LEE, APRIL 1941

"ILL-HOUSED, ILL-CLAD, ILL-NOURISHED"

Scavenging at the city dump, Ambridge, Pennsylvania.

PHOTO BY ARTHUR ROTHSTEIN, JULY 1938

The first hard times I remember came in 1933, when I was in the 8th grade," one boy recalled. "Travis and Son shut down and for six months Dad didn't draw a penny. . . . Then we were really up against it. . . . I remember lying in bed one night and thinking. All at once I realized something. We were poor. Lord! It was weeks before I could get over that."

What was it like to be poor in Depression America—to be young and needy at the worst of times? "In this nation," said President Franklin D. Roosevelt, "I see millions of citizens—a substantial part of the whole population—who at this very moment are denied the greater part of . . . the necessities of life. I see one-third of a nation ill-housed, ill-clad, ill-nourished."

By 1933, when Roosevelt entered office, the Great Depression was at its worst. Factories lay idle. Farmers burned crops they couldn't sell. Banks had stopped lending money to investors, merchants, and homeowners because they could not collect on loans they had already made. Worried depositors lined up to withdraw their savings, money they believed was safely stored deep inside steel bank vaults. But their cash had disappeared. It had been wiped out by the banks' risky loans.

Thousands of banks across the country failed, closing their doors for good when they could not pay off their depositors. People in all walks of life saw their life's savings vanish overnight. Even children lost the money they had deposited so conscientiously every week, penny by penny, through savings programs at their schools.

Unemployment had reached a record high. One out of every four Americans who wanted work could not find it. Thirty-four million men, women, and children—28 percent of the population at that time—had no income at all.

The Depression widened the gap between America's haves and have-nots. Many children and teenagers belonged to families that were comfortably well off and were not badly hurt by the economic crisis. But millions of kids grew up poor. Some children lived under conditions we associate today with impoverished developing nations. They could only dream of a world in which childhood is a time of innocence and play.

"We owe the landlord, the grocer—everybody," said a jobless steelworker. "My kids can't go to school. They don't have shoes."

President Franklin D. Roosevelt. When he took office on March 4, 1933, the Depression was at its worst.

When parents—almost always the father—lost their livelihood, the family might not be able to put enough food on the table. Government relief agencies helped feed the poorest families and held starvation at bay, and yet many people went hungry. Secretary of Labor Frances Perkins warned in 1933 that one out of every five preschool and school children was suffering from malnutrition.

"For a whole week one time we didn't have anything to eat but potatoes," one boy remembered. "Another time my brother went around to the grocery stores and got them to give him meat for his dog—only he didn't have any dog. We ate that dog meat with the potatoes. . . . I went to school hungry and came home to a house where there wasn't any [heat]. . . .

"Every now and then my brother or Dad would find some sort of odd job to do, or the other brother in Chicago would send us a little something. Then we'd go wild over food. We'd eat four times a day and between meals. We just couldn't help ourselves. The sight and smell of food sort of made us crazy, I guess."

In Depression America, "ill-housed" meant that many poor folks could not stay warm, keep food cold, or take a bath. According to a 1934 survey, 42 percent of city homes and apartments and 92 percent of farm dwellings had no central heating. In the nation as a whole, 27 percent of homes lacked

An old farmhouse stands on badly eroded land. The small child's bent legs are deformed by rickets, a disease caused by malnutrition.
PHOTO BY MARION POST WOLCOTT, DECEMBER 1938

Christmas dinner at a farmhouse near Smithfield, Iowa. Dinner consisted of potatoes, cabbage, and pie.

PHOTO BY RUSSELL LEE,
DECEMBER 1936

Time for a bath, Oklahoma City, Oklahoma.

PHOTO BY RUSSELL LEE,
JULY 1939

refrigeration equipment, 31 percent had no running water, 32 percent had an outdoor toilet or privy, and 39 percent did not have a bathtub or shower.

"We have lived in this house for sixteen years and we do not *yet* have a bathtub," a young Chicago woman told Eleanor Roosevelt. "I am the oldest of seven children, and my father works for the WPA [Works Progress Administration]. With his salary and the small one I make you can readily see that it would take forever for us to put a tub in. It has been my dream for sixteen years to have a tub put into our house, but I just can't make it come true."

As the nation's First Lady, Mrs. Roosevelt received thousands of letters from the Depression's youngest victims—poor children and teenagers who told her about their problems and often asked for her help. They requested small personal loans so they could stay in school ("I solemnly pledge to pay you back within 2 yrs"); asked for clothing they would not be ashamed to wear ("it just makes my heart ache to know that I can't even afford to dress decent"); wished for holiday gifts their families could not afford ("my poor mother will not be able to get my little sister and brother a doll or toy for Christmas so if your little grandchildren have any little things from last year I will be thankful to see you send them to us").

"Though we are poor," wrote a girl from North Carolina, "we try to hold off embarrassment, for you know it is 'hard to be broke, and harder to admit it.'"

African Americans, especially, were hurt by the Depression. Black

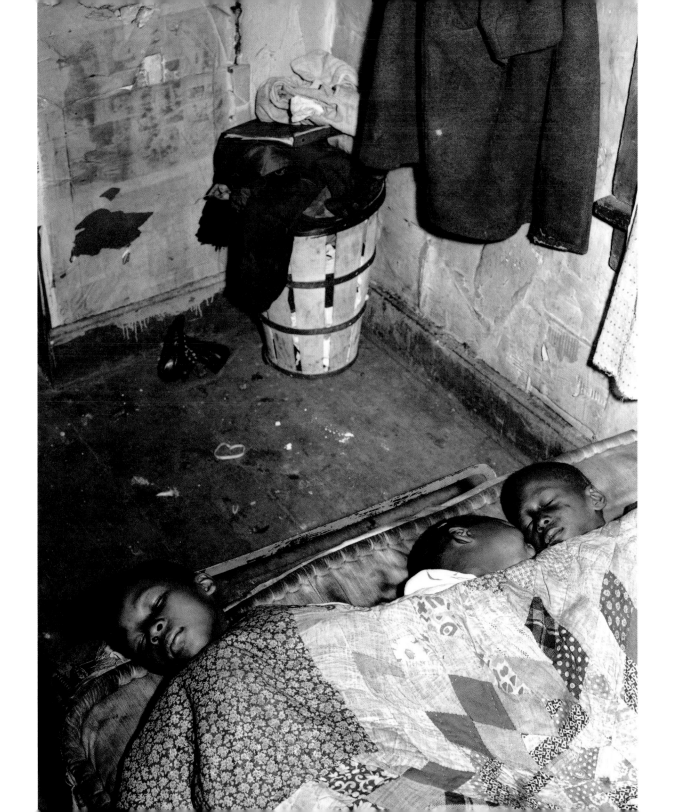

workers were usually the first to be laid off when times were tough. And black families had a hard time finding decent housing in the nation's segregated cities. They were forced to live in rundown neighborhoods, often in rickety tenements, where landlords charged exorbitant rents. Compared with the 20 to 25 percent of their income that white families generally paid for rent, black families in New York City's Harlem paid 40 to 50 percent. More than half of those families had to take in lodgers to make ends meet. Crowded living conditions were common; entire families frequently slept in one room.

As unemployment spread and businesses failed, many people had to give up their homes. A family would use up its savings, then drop its insurance policies, then pawn jewelry and clothes, and finally sell the furniture. When they could no longer make mortgage payments or meet the rent, they would have to move, often losing a house that was partly paid for.

In Philadelphia, children at a nursery school made up an eviction game. They would pile all their toy furniture in one corner of the room, then pick it up and move it to another corner. "We ain't got no money for rent," one child told their teacher, "so's we've moved into a new house. Then we got the constable [sheriff] on us, so we's moving again."

Older kids knew that eviction was no game, and they shared their parents' distress. A girl from Brooklyn, whose family couldn't pay the rent and was about to be evicted, confided to Eleanor Roosevelt: "My father tries to be gay about it saying as lightly as possible 'Who cares. Who wants to live

Children sleeping in a tenement apartment on Chicago's strictly segregated South Side.

Photo by Russell Lee, April 1941

here anyway?' But under all his jokes I can see he is suffering terrible my pop is very sensitive."

A dispossessed family might move to a poorer neighborhood. If all else failed, they might seek refuge as squatters in one of the shantytowns that were springing up in vacant lots and on the outskirts of every city. The shelters in these ramshackle settlements were built of whatever came to hand—scraps of cardboard and wood, packing crates, fence posts, flattened tin cans, sheets of canvas, anything that could keep out the wind and rain. Everyone called the settlements "Hoovervilles," a bitter tribute to former president Herbert Hoover, who was widely blamed for doing too little too late to head off the Depression.

Shacks and shanties provide homes for destitute families in this ramshackle Hooverville outside Seattle, Washington, March 1933.

New York City was sprinkled with Hoovervilles. "Along the Hudson, below Riverside Drive," author Robert Bendiner recalled, "I daily passed the tarpaper huts of a Hooverville, where scores of families lived the lives of reluctant gypsies, cooking whatever they had to cook over open fires within sight of passengers on the double-deck . . . buses. Dozens of such colonies had sprung up in the city—along the two rivers, in the empty lots of the Bronx, and on the flats of Brooklyn, but not nearly enough to accommodate the swelling army of the jobless and the dispossessed."

Not all Hoovervilles were in or near cities. "Grandma and Grandpa would get as many as we could in the car," Inez Williamson recalled. "At that time there was [a] Hooverville on the White River and they'd take us down there. And those people, well, if you'd see something like that you'll be thankful that you had a home. They had all built shacks on the water. . . . [Grandma] would say, 'Now, if you kids don't appreciate what you got, just take a look at those children. They don't even have your sweets and your fruits but maybe once a month. . . .' And so it really made us stop and think."

Many middle-class families managed to get through the Depression by stretching every available dollar. "With no dependable income, we cut back on everything possible," wrote Robert Hastings, recalling his childhood days in Marion, Illinois. "We stopped the evening paper, turned off the city water and cleaned out our well, sold our four-door Model T touring car with the snap-on side curtains, stopped ice and milk delivery, and discon-

23

nected our gas range. . . . There was no telephone to disconnect, as we didn't have one to start with!

"Looking back, I find it amazing what we did without. A partial list would include toothpaste (we used [baking] soda), toilet paper (we used the catalog), newspaper and magazine subscriptions, soft drinks, potato chips and snacks, paper clips, rubber bands, and restaurant meals. . . . We sent no greeting cards except maybe half a dozen at Christmas."

Giving up the family car was often the cruelest blow of all. Millions of Americans had purchased their first automobiles during the prosperous 1920s. New highways had sprung up all across the country, along with filling stations, garages, and billboards, changing the face of America forever. But when the Depression arrived, many drivers decided that they could no longer afford to keep the family car on the road.

This twelve-year-old girl in Harlingen, Texas, does the family laundry on an old-fashioned washboard.
PHOTO BY RUSSELL LEE, FEBRUARY 1939

As families exhausted their savings, housewives who had never worked outside the home took in washing and ironing while their husbands looked for work.
PHOTO BY RUSSELL LEE, OKLAHOMA CITY, AUGUST 1939

WASHINGS
AND
IORNINGS
DONE HERE

"I was a sophomore in high school then," said one boy, "and probably had as good an idea as most kids my age of what was going on, but I don't think I really understood just how tight things were with us until one Saturday afternoon I came home and found my Dad decommissioning the old Essex [touring car], which was just like one of the family to us.

"I helped him take out the battery and drain the crankcase and radiator and take out the plugs. Then we put a little oil in the cylinders and jacked her up on blocks and took off the wheels. Dad was not much of a mechanic and neither was I, but we knew what to do well enough. Everybody did. By then, putting the car on blocks had already become an American ritual—sort of a public admission that the pinch was on. It was a very solemn affair. I remember saying to my Dad that we ought to have the priest over to say something in Latin, but Dad didn't think that was very funny. You don't joke about anything as serious as jacking up the car."

Main Street, Plain City, Ohio. During hard times, many people gave up the family car.
PHOTO BY BEN SHAHN, AUGUST 1938

IN AND OUT OF SCHOOL

A schoolgirl in New Madrid County, Missouri.

PHOTO BY RUSSELL LEE, AUGUST 1938

Gordon Parks, who became a noted photographer and filmmaker, was a sixteen-year-old living on his own in St. Paul, Minnesota, and working his way through high school. He had a job as a bellboy at the Minnesota Club, an exclusive establishment for wealthy businessmen. He worked full-time during the summer of 1929, and in September he switched to part-time so he could begin classes at Central High.

When he arrived at work on a Wednesday afternoon in October, he found a puzzling notice tacked to the bulletin board in the employees' locker room. It read: "Because of unforeseen circumstances, some personnel will be laid off the first of next month. Those directly affected will be notified in due time. The management."

"I changed into my [uniform]," Parks recalled in his autobiography, "wondering what had happened.

"By Thursday [October 24] the entire world knew. 'Market Crashes—Panic Hits Nation!' one headline blared. The newspapers were full of it, and I read everything I could get my hands on, gathering in the full meaning of such terms as Black Thursday, deflation and depression. I couldn't imagine such financial disaster touching my small world; it surely concerned only the rich. But by the first week of November I too knew differently; along with millions of others across the nation, I was without a job. All that next week I searched for any kind of work that would prevent my leaving school. Again it was, 'We're firing, not hiring.' 'Sorry, sonny, nothing doing here.' Finally, on the seventh of November, I went to school and cleaned out my locker, knowing it was impossible to stay on. A piercing chill was in the air as I walked back to the rooming house."

By the end of 1930, hard times had forced some three million young people between the ages of seven and seventeen to leave school. They dropped out because, like Gordon Parks, they could not support themselves while in school; because they had to find jobs to help support their families; because their schools had no money to provide free textbooks or transportation; or, in many cases, because they lacked shoes or warm clothes for the winter months, and their families were too poor to buy them.

Schools across the country were crippled by the economic crisis. As people's incomes fell, so did the tax revenues that support public education.

To save money, thousands of elementary schools, junior highs, and high schools shortened the school year, often to just six or seven months. Some schools opened their doors only three days a week. And some shut down completely.

A disheartened fourteen-year-old farm girl wrote to her cousin: "With the school closed (I feel like crying every time I see it with the doors and windows boarded up) I'll be too old before I'm ready to go to high school. Do you think that you could get on without a school or even a set of books?"

Black schools in the segregated South had always been poorly funded. Now they suffered the most drastic cutbacks. In Alabama an elementary school for black children, which normally ran four months a year, closed entirely during the 1932–33 school year. After that, it averaged less than three months of classes each year.

Teachers everywhere were laid off. Those who kept their jobs saw their salaries slashed, and some worked for months without being paid. With fewer teachers, class sizes increased, doubling in some places from twenty-five or thirty kids in a classroom to fifty or more.

In Chicago thousands of teachers stormed city hall to demand their back pay. Then, supported by students and parents, they paraded with their picket signs through downtown streets. When the protesters invaded several banks, disrupting business and demanding that bankers lend the city money to pay teachers' salaries, the police moved in on foot and horseback. "In a

Some communities could not afford to operate a school bus. These kids in Red House, West Virginia, are transported to school in the back of a truck.
PHOTO BY BEN SHAHN, OCTOBER 1935

moment," one newspaper reported, "unpaid policemen were cracking their clubs against the heads of unpaid school teachers."

Many poor kids went to school hungry every morning. A Chicago principal told his teachers, "Whenever you have a discipline case, ask this question first, What has he had for breakfast? Which usually brings out the fact that he has had nothing at all."

Somehow, Chicago's unpaid teachers managed to come to the aid of their hungry students. *The New York Times* reported in 1931 that teachers and principals in Chicago public schools were providing lunches for 11,000 kids with money from their own pockets.

In the impoverished mining towns of the Appalachians, entire families were living on dandelions, pokeweed, and blackberries. It was reported that some children grew so hungry, they chewed on their hands until they drew blood. One child who looked ill when she arrived at school was told by her teacher to go home and get something to eat. "I can't," she replied. "It's my sister's turn to eat."

Philip Levine, who became an award-winning poet, wrote about his Depression-era schooldays in Detroit. When he entered the second grade, he began to notice "for the first time" that some of his classmates were desperately poor, while others came from families that were comfortably well off. "Not once did I go off to school without a sacked lunch," he wrote. Many other students "had nothing to eat [at lunchtime] except the free carton of milk provided by the school. By the age of ten I'd decided that it was easier

Children in Norfolk, Virginia, protesting against the school board's treatment of African American teachers, June 1939. One sign reads: "We want our teachers equally prepared and equally paid."

*A schoolboy reading,
New Madrid County, Missouri.*

PHOTO BY RUSSELL LEE,
AUGUST 1938

to walk the mile back to our apartment and eat my lunch in privacy than to bear the envious glances of my classmates."

Levine also noticed "how differently we students dressed. . . . There was one boy who wore . . . elegant sweaters in subtle tones of brown and fawn; even his checked socks were in matching colors. . . . This boy, Milton Journey, was always driven to school in a long white LaSalle convertible. . . . On winter days, after school, Milton would wait in his long blue overcoat inside the main doors until his mother stopped and honked from her sedan. Milton would toss back his straight blond hair, shrug, and go out into the weather to accept his privileges.

"Another boy, Fred Batten, wore no socks, and often that winter the skin of his ankles was raw and swollen. One day he caught me looking at

Drinking from the school water pump, New Madrid County, Missouri.

PHOTO BY RUSSELL LEE, AUGUST 1938

his bare ankles, and he turned away from me in silence. I began to notice several other boys and girls who bore those same 'wounds' at wrists and ankles, and I did my best not to stare at them."

Philip often walked home from school with a classmate, Martin Peters: "Suddenly, during a particularly cold week in January, Martin stopped coming to school. I didn't see him for three weeks. The word was he was suffering from pneumonia, but when he returned to class he shared his secret. His mother had been keeping him home because he had no heavy jacket or coat. His father was out of work, the gas bill had not been paid, so the heat had been shut off. Martin had spent most days in bed, under the covers, listening to the radio."

"I find so many children [who] do not get to go to school because they

simply haven't a rag that they can leave home in," observed an Arkansas relief worker.

Children whose families had been impoverished by the Depression did not want to feel like outsiders among their more fortunate friends and classmates. They didn't want to be embarrassed or ashamed because they couldn't afford the dressy clothes worn by everyone else at proms, graduation exercises, and other important school social events. Graduation was an especially tough time for poor students who had worked for years to complete their schooling. Along with acceptable clothes, they needed money to buy school rings, yearbooks, pins, class photos, and all the other symbols of their achievement. Because many of their classmates could afford these graduation expenses, while they themselves couldn't even dress properly, they dreaded the approach of the graduation season, and when it arrived, they felt heartsick.

"My folks are poor and cannot afford to buy my graduation clothes," a despondent Oklahoma girl told Eleanor Roosevelt. "It takes every cent they get to buy food. . . . No one on earth knows how my heart aches. I have been looking forward to my graduation for a long time and studying hard to make it."

During the Depression, only about 10 percent of college-age Americans were able to attend college. Today, more than 50 percent of high-school graduates go on to college.

Reading on the front steps of the one-room Lincoln Bench School, Malheur County, Oregon.
Photo by Dorothea Lange, October 1939

KIDS AT WORK

The hardships faced by Depression families placed heavy responsibilities on the shoulders of the young. Children had to grow up fast. They were called on to contribute to the meager family income by working full-time or part-time, assuming they could find a job.

"There are no advantages in staying in school for my children," one parent said, "for we could not keep them there long enough to [become] teachers or get enough education to do some other professional work, so it is better for them to get to work early."

"It's better to go to work and bring money home," agreed a mill worker's son, who had six brothers and sisters living at home. "Schools are only for the rich. Poor people must work for their living."

Picking hops on an Oregon farm. This eleven-year-old migrant worker started picking at five A.M. The photo was taken at noon, when the temperature was 105 degrees.

PHOTO BY DOROTHEA LANGE, POLK COUNTY, OREGON, AUGUST 1939

Often it was the sixteen- and seventeen-year-olds who dropped out of school to find work. But it wasn't unusual to find much younger children laboring long hours for little pay. Fourteen-year-old boys worked in coal mines, twelve-year-old girls in knitting factories. Among migrant farm workers, children as young as five or six labored in the fields beside their parents, working from sunup to sundown.

Some states had enacted laws prohibiting or limiting child labor, but for the most part those laws were weak and enforcement was lax. At the beginning of the Depression, there was no national child-labor law that applied equally to all American children.

In 1930, according to the census, two and a quarter million boys and girls between the ages of ten and eighteen were working in factories, canneries, mines, and farms. Tens of thousands of other children *under* the age of ten, who were laboring on farms, as street peddlers, and in home workshops, were not counted by the census. Because kids could be hired for lower wages than grownups, they often replaced adults who had been laid off. A child's wages might make up the entire family income. "I don't expect I'll ever get back to school," said a thirteen-year-old girl who was working in the same cotton garment factory that had laid off her father.

"If our eyes are open we cannot fail to see child labor all over the United States today," reported two Smith College economists, Katharine DuPre Lumpkin and Dorothy Wolff Douglas, in their 1937 book, *Child Workers in America.* "In agriculture, in street trades, at industrial home-

High-school girls in Nampa, Idaho, waiting to be trucked to the fields in pea-picking season.

Photo by Russell Lee, June 1941

work, in factories, in the service trades, in stores, as servants in private houses, children are at work. Not only boys and girls of 14 and over are at these tasks. At many of them thousands of little children not more than 13 and some as young as 6 can today be found."

A girl who started work when she was fourteen described her daily routine: "At 5:30 it is time for me to get up. . . . I hurriedly eat my breakfast, and I am ready to go to work. It is a chilly winter morning, but I know it will be hot in the mill. I start on my three mile walk to the factory. As I walk, I see others hurrying to work. I look at the older people and wonder if they, too, feel the resentment every morning that I do, or if as the years go by their spirits are deadened.

"I arrive at the factory. The sight that I dread to see meets my eyes: the line of unemployed people waiting for the boss to come and hoping for work."

Kids who were able to stay in school found a variety of part-time jobs. They were employed as newspaper carriers, babysitters, store clerks, and delivery boys. One boy from a hard-pressed Michigan home delivered newspapers in the afternoon, ushered at a theater in the evening, and worked at a gas station on weekends. He also helped his mother at home while his father was away searching for a job. A North Carolina girl went to school mornings and worked at the local cotton mill in the evenings "because I wanted to help my parents and not be a burden to them."

Vincent Ferrara managed to stay in college by working in his family's New York City pizzeria. "If I wasn't there, I was in school or I was doing my homework," he recalled. "Saturday night was a busy night, so was Sunday. I saved my tip money, and I worked in the church hall for thirty-seven dollars a month, and all put together enabled me to pay for my tuition at Fordham. I went during the day, and at night I was in the store. I did my homework on the rear table."

Some teenagers found a novel, if dangerous, way to make money when a tree-sitting craze swept the country. A boy would climb to the highest branch of a tall tree and sit there for days on end, hoping to break a tree-sitting record and earn some cash from donations dropped into a coin box placed at the foot of the tree. Local merchants often paid tree-sitters to

A young worker at a cotton mill in Taftville, Connecticut.

Photo by Jack Delano, November 1940

A girl picker at a cranberry bog in
Burlington County, New Jersey.

PHOTO BY ARTHUR ROTHSTEIN, OCTOBER 1938

Bootblacks in Market Square, Waco, Texas.

PHOTO BY RUSSELL LEE,
NOVEMBER 1939

advertise their wares, and some boys made extra money by selling their autographs.

A teenage couple could get some money by entering a dance marathon. These events also became a 1930s craze. Spectators paid to watch young couples dance hour after hour until they dropped to the floor, exhausted. Those who stayed on their feet the longest earned a little prize money.

Young people who managed to save enough money to pay tuition often went to vocational schools, where they trained to become secretaries, bookkeepers, mechanics, beauticians, refrigeration technicians, and even commercial pilots. But no matter how impressive their skills, they had a hard time finding work. The depressed job market of the 1930s hit the young especially hard. In 1934–35, unemployment rates among sixteen- to

A young boy packing shingles at a Jefferson, Texas, lumber mill.
PHOTO BY RUSSELL LEE, APRIL 1939

A delivery boy in
Caruthersville, Missouri.

PHOTO BY RUSSELL LEE, AUGUST 1938

twenty-four-year-olds hovered around 50 percent. In New York City, nearly 80 percent of sixteen-year-olds who were out of school and looking for work could not find jobs.

"Maybe you don't know what it's like to come home and have everyone looking at you," one teenager complained, "and you know they're thinking, even if they don't say it, 'He didn't find a job.' It gets terrible. You just don't want to come home."

Among black youths, the unemployment situation was critical. Although Northern blacks did not face the rigid segregation of the Deep South, job discrimination was still the rule in Northern cities. Black workers of any age were always "the last hired and the first fired," as the saying goes. And jobs previously held by unskilled black workers were now being grabbed by whites willing to work as waiters, garbage collectors, and domestic servants.

At first, none of the massive government programs designed to ease the pain of the Depression did much to meet the needs of an estimated three million young people who were said to be "out of work, out of school, and out of luck." The Civilian Conservation Corps (CCC), established in 1933, hired unemployed young men between the ages of seventeen and twenty-eight and put them to work in national forests and parks. They planted trees, fought fires, and improved beaches and campgrounds. It was hailed as a successful program, but it excluded young women and did nothing to help students.

Eleanor Roosevelt insisted that the nation's youth deserved the government's help as much as any other group. Because she received an overwhelming volume of mail, she was unable to respond in the very personal ways the letter writers hoped. Instead, as First Lady, she used her considerable influence and popularity to crusade for expanded federal aid to poor children and teens. "I have moments of real terror when I think we might be losing this generation," she said. "We have got to bring these young people into the active life of the community."

Mrs. Roosevelt pressed government leaders to set up a special agency for young Americans who were still in school. Finally, she persuaded her

Eleanor Roosevelt at White Top Mountain, Virginia, August 1933. During her first year in the White House, she received more than 300,000 letters, many of them from children.

Student assistants at the Greenwood Negro Library, Leflore County, Mississippi, May 1936. NYA work grants helped students like these stay in school.

husband, Franklin D. Roosevelt, to issue an executive order in 1935 creating the National Youth Administration (NYA). And she insisted that the new agency administer aid without discrimination, so that it reached blacks as well as whites, girls as well as boys.

The NYA provided grants to help Depression-squeezed young people stay in school. Under this program, high-school and college students were paid to work part-time in libraries and as research assistants. For many of these students, an NYA job meant the difference between staying in school and dropping out. Between 1936 and 1943, more than two million low-income students were able to continue their education through NYA work-study jobs. Another two and a half million youths were employed by the NYA in its after-school work-relief projects.

The NYA had its critics. They charged that the program undermined the initiative and self-reliance of the nation's youth. Segregationists objected

because black youths were included in NYA projects. Despite this opposition, the NYA became one of the most popular of all federal government programs. A teenager from Pittsburgh who had been hired by the program wrote: "Words cannot express my gratitude to our President, who had made this [employment] possible for me and thousands of others."

Years later, people who had grown up during the worst times of the Great Depression looked back with a certain pride. They had missed out on some of the carefree years that are the special gift of youth, but they had gained, they felt, a sense of heightened self-confidence and an understanding of the needs of others. Hard times had propelled them into the adult world much sooner than they might have wished, yet they had discovered within themselves strengths and skills that would last throughout their lives.

"It was an enormously hard life," author Margot Hentoff recalled. "But there was also a sense of great satisfaction in being a child with valuable work to do and, being able to do it well, [able] to function in this world."

Stacking crates of cranberries, Burlington County, New Jersey.
PHOTO BY ARTHUR ROTHSTEIN, OCTOBER 1938

"OKIE, GO HOME!"

On the road: A migrant boy looks out from the back of the car as the family travels through Muskogee County, Oklahoma, in search of work.

PHOTO BY RUSSELL LEE, JUNE 1939

During the 1930s, about a quarter of all Americans still lived on farms (compared with fewer than 2 percent today). For millions of children growing up on those Depression-era farms, it was a time of hard work, little money, and learning to do without.

"I have to get up every morning at five and milk six cows and carry in the water and cut the wood and then eat breakfast and go to school," a North Carolina farm boy wrote to Eleanor Roosevelt. That boy walked four miles to catch the school bus that took him the rest of the way to his high school in Bryson City. "When it rains I can't go to school," he added, "and part of the time I am late."

"I have done a boy's work ever since I was five years old," wrote a fourteen-year-old Texas farm girl. "This week I have been breaking land with a sulky [one-horse] plow and three mules. . . . When I read how you [Mrs. Roosevelt] get $3,000 for each radio broadcast, I can't help but think how unjust the world is."

American farmers were the world's most productive, yet they, too, experienced hard times during the Depression. Because they produced far more than they could sell, huge surpluses piled up. The prices of farm products dropped steadily, while taxes on a farmer's land and the prices he paid for necessities did not. As a result, the average farmer was paying out more than he took in. Hundreds of thousands of farmers had borrowed money to buy their land and equipment. When they couldn't make payments to the bank, they lost everything through foreclosures and bankruptcy sales. Farm after farm went on the auction block.

Slim Collier recalled the day his father took him to a farm foreclosure near Waterloo, Iowa: "It was the first of March when they were forced off, and all their household goods were sold. Even family pictures. They went for five cents, ten cents apiece. Quite a few kids were brought by their parents, partly by morbid fascination, partly by sympathy—well, there was something going on. In those days of no TV, no radio in some places, an event was an event."

There were farmers who resisted. "If they come to take my farm, I'm going to fight," one man was quoted as saying. "I'd rather be killed outright than die by starvation. But before I die, I'm going to set fire to

A sharecropper and his family at home, Hale County, Alabama.

PHOTO BY WALKER EVANS, ABOUT 1935

my crops, I'm going to burn my house! I'm going to p'izen [poison] my cattle."

Almost half the nation's farmers did not own any farmland. They lived on and worked land owned by others, and they paid rent in cash or with a share of the crops they raised. This system was especially common in the South, where more than a million poor blacks and poor whites labored as tenants and sharecroppers with little prospect of ever actually owning a farm or making a decent living.

When other kids were just starting kindergarten or the first grade, these farmers' children began working in the fields beside their parents. A glimpse of a boy named Tom, the son of a black sharecropper in Alabama, comes from a field study conducted by Smith College economists Katharine DuPre Lumpkin and Dorothy Wolff Douglas.

Tom was twelve years old when Lumpkin and Douglas visited the two-room cabin where he lived with his father, mother, and three other children "old enough to 'make hands' [pick cotton]." All of them worked for the landowner, along with other sharecropper families living on the same cotton plantation.

"Tom gets up, or is pulled out of bed, at four o'clock in summer, by his older brother, who is quicker than he to hear the landlord's bell," the economists wrote. "Work for the entire plantation force is 'from can see to can't

A sharecropper's son at work in the field, New Madrid County, Missouri.
PHOTO BY RUSSELL LEE, MAY 1938

see' (i.e., from daylight to dark), and the bell is their commanding time-piece. . . .

"Tom is a good steady chopper and can do over half a man's work. At picking he can do two-thirds. Peter, aged 9, does considerably less than that. . . . All the children pick with both hands, and by the end of the first season the lifetime rhythm of pluck, pluck, drop-in-the-bag is long since established. But now that Tom is taller he has to stoop so much, or move along on his knees, while the littlest fellows scramble by with 'hardly a bend to them.'"

Tom had attended "part of three grades. The Negro school in his district runs four months 'normally' (the white school runs six); but in the year 1932–33 it closed altogether, and since then it has been averaging less than three months. Besides, cotton-picking season in Alabama runs well into November, and after that it is often too cold to go to school without shoes. So from January on Tom and Peter have been taking turns in one pair."

Because tenant farmers and sharecroppers worked on land owned by someone else, they could be evicted at the landowner's whim. And that's what happened during the Depression years. Huge farm surpluses were driving down prices. Warehouses were stacked to the rafters with cotton and other crops that could be sold only at a loss. In an effort to reduce the surpluses, the federal government began to pay landowners to stop farming on some of their land. While the program helped prop up prices, it had the unintended effect of uprooting tenant and sharecropper families. If a landowner had no crop to plant or harvest, then he had no need for share-

An evicted sharecropper's son.

Evicted sharecroppers parked along the highway in New Madrid County, Missouri.

PHOTOS BY ARTHUR ROTHSTEIN, JANUARY 1939

croppers or tenants. The gradual introduction of labor-saving tractors also eliminated many farm jobs.

Throughout the 1930s, tens of thousands of dispossessed tenants and sharecroppers were evicted from their homes. They joined the nation's drifting population of migrant farm laborers—some four million men, women, and children who harvested crops on commercial farms from Maine to California.

Meanwhile, as if the nation's economic crisis weren't bad enough, nature dealt a crippling blow to farmers in the nation's heartland. One of the worst droughts in memory gripped the Great Plains, from North Dakota to Texas. Along with the lowest rainfall ever recorded in the region, a succession of blistering heat waves baked the plains. Ponds, streams, and reservoirs dried up. Crops withered in the fields. In some places, staggering livestock, weak and wild-eyed from hunger, bawling helplessly for water, dropped dead in their tracks.

Poor farming practices and overgrazing by cattle and sheep had exhausted much of the region's topsoil. As a result, the 1930s drought was unusually destructive. Prairie winds swept down on this loose, dry soil, scooped it up, and carried it into the air as enormous choking clouds of dust. Terrifying wind-driven dust storms called "black blizzards" boiled up from the parched land and rolled across entire states, darkening the sky, advancing at fifty miles an hour as thousands of fleeing geese, ducks, and smaller birds raced for their lives ahead of the approaching storm.

The dust was so finely powdered, and the winds that carried it so strong, it could sandblast the paint off the side of a house. "The impact is like a shovelful of fine sand flung against the face," wrote Avis D. Carlson in *The New Republic*. "People caught in their own yards grope for the doorstep. Cars come to a standstill, for no light in the world can penetrate that swirling muck. . . . The darkness is like the end of the world. . . . We live with the dust, eat it, sleep with it, watch it strip us of possessions and the hope of possessions."

The region that was hit hardest—parts of Kansas, Nebraska, Colorado, Oklahoma, Texas, and New Mexico—became known as the Dust Bowl. Roving reporter Ernie Pyle visited the area in the summer of 1936. "If you would like to have your heart broken, just come out here," he wrote. "This is the dust-storm country. It is the saddest land I have ever seen."

Advancing at fifty miles an hour, a gigantic dust storm is about to engulf this ranch near Boise City, Oklahoma, April 1935.

Caught in a raging dust storm, 1934.

An orchard covered with sand following a dust storm, Cimarron County, Oklahoma.
PHOTO BY ARTHUR ROTHSTEIN, APRIL 1936

Many farm families managed to stick it out until the drought ended and the rains returned in 1938. But thousands of others, "baked out and broke," their crops and pasture land ruined, felt they had no choice but to abandon the farms and ranches that had been in their families for generations. As many as three and a half million people may have left the Plains states during the Depression years—no one knows the exact number. Some counties lost half their population. "The land just blew away," said a Kansas preacher. "We had to go somewhere."

Many of these Dust Bowl refugees headed for California. Families piled into ancient cars and trucks, everything they owned roped or wired to their vehicles, shy, excited children crowded into backseats and truck beds as they sputtered down dusty highways leading to an unknown land. The refugees came from several different states, but when they arrived on the

West Coast, most people figured they must have come from failed farms in Oklahoma, the area hardest hit by the dust storms. No matter where they were from, they were all lumped together simply as "Okies."

They had heard glowing reports about California's sunny climate and fertile soil, and many of them hoped to set up new farms. But when they reached the Golden State, they found that they had little chance of ever owning land there. Most California farms were not the small family homesteads the migrants had known back in the Midwest. Instead, they were huge commercial operations, factory farms owned by big companies.

Some of the Dust Bowl refugees found places for themselves in and around West Coast cities and towns, where they joined family members or friends already settled. But a large number, those who had no choice, became migrant farm laborers, constantly on the move as they followed California's crops from season to season. Since there were more workers than jobs, migrant families had no choice but to labor in the fields for poverty wages. The average field hand worked sixteen hours a day, seven days a week, and earned four dollars a week—when work was available.

The children of migrant workers were even worse off than tenant and sharecropper kids, because often they had no permanent home. They moved with their parents from farm to farm, living in shabby, overcrowded labor camps provided by farmers or built by the workers themselves. These settlements were called Little Oklahomas or Okievilles. They were also known as ditch camps, because they clustered at the sides of roads along which ran filthy irrigation ditches.

A migrant family drives across the Arizona desert. No matter how decrepit, an automobile was a prized possession. It allowed migrants to travel in search of work.
PHOTO BY DOROTHEA LANGE, MAY 1937

"The typical migratory worker's accommodation consists of a tar-paper shanty with no plumbing and no floor," wrote Paul Y. Anderson in *The Nation*. "He must furnish his own blankets and rustle his own firewood. At the very large ranches he buys his groceries from the company store and the prices are high. . . . The children in these wretched families are seldom able to obtain any schooling, and their mortality rate is appalling."

There was never enough water in the camps. There were no toilets other

This migrant workers' camp in California adjoins an irrigation ditch. Most of these makeshift settlements had no sanitary facilities.

PHOTO BY DOROTHEA LANGE, NOVEMBER 1936

than a rare outhouse, so the nearby irrigation ditch was everyone's toilet. Illness, disease, and malnutrition were common. During an inspection tour in California's San Joaquin Valley, a social worker found "dozens of children with horribly sore eyes; many cases of cramps, diarrhea, and dysentery; fever, colds, and sore throats."

Along with illness, poverty, and dreadful living conditions, Okies were targets of the hostility and contempt that often confront outsiders, and that had been heaped on generations of immigrant Mexican, Filipino, Chinese, and Japanese workers who had labored in the fields before them. The ragged, disheveled migrants and their grimy, coughing children were blamed

The home of an agricultural day laborer near Vian, Oklahoma.
PHOTO BY RUSSELL LEE, JUNE 1939

for their poverty. They were "shiftless trash who live like dogs," said a California physician.

Author John Steinbeck captured the hardships suffered by the Okies in his best-selling novel *The Grapes of Wrath*, published in 1939, which portrays the Joad family's journey from their foreclosed farm in Oklahoma to the promised land of California. Winner of the Pulitzer Prize for fiction, and recognized today as a landmark of American literature, the novel was condemned at the time by California fruit growers who objected to Steinbeck's graphic depiction of the Okies' plight, calling the novel "vile propaganda." Growers burned the book in public. And they pressured local bookstores to remove it from their shelves.

Children suffered the most from the prejudice aimed at Okies. Many kids had missed a lot of schooling because their parents were on the move, and some couldn't read or write long after other kids their age had learned how. When they showed up at the local public schools without shoes, wearing dresses made of chicken-feed sacks or baggy overalls held up by ropes, their better-dressed classmates made fun of them. In the schoolyard, they heard shouts of "Okie, go home!" Some teachers decided that the shy, embarrassed Okie kids were stupid or retarded. At one school, teachers had the newcomers sit on the floor in back of the room, while their classsmates, the children of local ranchers and townspeople, sat at well-equipped desks.

Conditions in California's farm-labor camps were so bad that the federal government introduced a program to provide decent living conditions

Migrant labor camps built by the federal government, like this one in California's Imperial Valley, provided decent living conditions.

Photo by Dorothea Lange, February 1939

67

for the migrants. Beginning in 1935, more than a dozen federal camps were constructed where families could move into clean one-room cabins or into large tents sitting on wooden platforms, and where they had access to flush toilets, hot showers, laundry facilities, and, in many camps, recreation halls.

Kids at a federal government resettlement camp near Marysville, California.
PHOTO BY DOROTHEA LANGE, SEPTEMBER 1935

Over the years, the Okie tents and cabins, and the shacks outside the federal camps, were replaced by more substantial housing. Gradually, the Little Oklahomas were absorbed into the towns and cities they bordered. And as the country mobilized for war in 1940, the vast majority of Okie migrants abandoned California's factory-farm fields for better-paying jobs in the war effort's booming defense plants.

Okie children stuck it out at the local schools and even helped build a special school of their own near Bakersfield. As they moved into the larger community, they became high-school teachers and principals, college professors, business executives, lawyers, research scientists, and engineers, among many other trades and professions.

Prejudice gave way to respect, and the term "Okie," coined by others as a term of abuse, became a badge of honor, an affirmation of strength, determination, and pride.

BOXCAR KIDS

Looking for an empty freight car near Bakersfield, California, April 1940.

A bunch of boys and young men have gathered at a railroad crossing. Some have packs strapped to their backs. Others are holding battered suitcases or have all their belongings tied up in bundles. They are waiting for a freight train.

They hear two sharp blasts from a locomotive's whistle; then the train comes rolling into view. As it approaches, they dart out from under bushes, from behind piles of junk, from the shadows of nearby houses. Running alongside the track, reaching out to grab the steel handrails on the sides of boxcars, they leap forward and pull themselves onto the moving train.

This was a familiar scene during the 1930s. "It was no trick for a swift, skinny kid to grab the rung of a ladder on a slow-moving freight, then climb

Boys hopping a freight, about 1935.

up on top or swing into an empty boxcar, going who knows where," John Gojack recalled. He had done exactly that when he was twelve years old.

John was part of what *Fortune* magazine called "the vast homeless horde," a restless legion of tramps and hoboes who took to the nation's rails and roads, hopping freights, thumbing rides, bumming meals as they roamed America. All cities and towns of any consequence had train stations and railroad yards in those days before commercial air travel, when people and goods went everywhere by train.

By late 1932, at least 250,000 of these Depression-era nomads were youths under the age of twenty-one. Many had been to high school, some to college. Others were barely into their teens, or like John Gojack, even younger. They had taken to the road for different reasons—because they had failed to find a job near home, or because they felt they were a burden to their families. Some had run away from families broken by the pressures of unemployment and poverty. Some had left with their families' blessings. And some had been lured from their Depression homes by pure wanderlust, by dreams of excitement and adventure. Whatever their backgrounds and hopes, they kept moving, always on the lookout for a meal, a place to sleep, and work they could do for pay.

Traveling in a boxcar between Bakersfield and Fresno, California, April 1940.

During the summers of 1932 and 1933, Thomas Minehan, a graduate student in sociology at the University of Minnesota, dressed as a hobo and rode the rails with boxcar kids. He reported his findings in a book called *Boy and Girl Tramps of America*. Minehan found that young people often traveled in pairs or groups for safety, especially if there were girls among them. It was hard to tell how many girls were riding the rails, because a large number of them traveled disguised as boys.

"Mobs of men got off every [freight] train," he wrote. "Many were not youths, but boys. And some were girls—children really—dressed in overalls or army breeches and boys' coats and sweaters—looking, except for their dirt and rags, like a Girl Scout club on an outing."

"In boxcars and [hobo camps] boys and girls are able to associate in large numbers and protect themselves. In the event of loneliness or illness, the boys and girls have friends to comfort and care for them. Fear of being alone, fear of being spied on and seized by the first cop who comes along is absent."

Some girls found being a female an advantage. "It was easier for a girl than a boy on the road," recalled Peggy DeHart, who was sixteen when she set out. "People bought us meals and gave us the change out of their pockets and I doubt that they would do that as readily for a boy."

Minehan asked each boy or girl he interviewed, "Why did you leave home?" Four out of five "stated definitely that hard times drove them away from home," he reported.

Armed with a rifle, a railroad company detective patrols a railroad bridge in Tulsa, Oklahoma.

Photo by John Vachon, October 1942

Most of the boxcar kids, Minehan found, had been on the road an average of fourteen months and had traveled within a radius of only five hundred miles from where they had started. They knew where to find the best shelters offering a square meal and a bed for the night, and also where the police and railroad detectives were most likely to hassle them. Many spent as much time walking along country roads as they did riding the rails or hitchhiking. They swapped stories about their travels, told each other where to catch the trains in and out of big towns, how to tell when a train was ready for departure, what part of the train to board.

"It was dangerous riding the freights," remembered Clarence Lee, a sharecropper's son who was sixteen years old at the time. "You had to be careful not to stumble or fall under the wheels when you climbed on the cars. You had to jump off at the right time too 'cause once the train picked up speed you had a hard time getting off. Sometimes you slept in a boxcar in a rail yard. Next morning when you woke up the train would be taking off with you. It was scary and dangerous but you had to do it to survive."

Accidents were common. One misstep could cost you your legs or your life. Thousands of young nomads were injured or crippled while boarding or leaving moving trains.

Run-ins with the "bulls"—railroad detectives—and with local police were also common. It was the job of the bulls, who patrolled with lanterns and rifles, to eject trespassers from railroad property. And many towns were just as unwelcoming, refusing to feed or shelter young wanderers for more than a day before sending them on their way. Officials in some places rounded them up, transported them to the city limits or the county line, and warned them not to return.

Helping newcomers climb aboard a freight car.

Waiting for a meal and a bed for the night at the city mission in Dubuque, Iowa.

PHOTO BY JOHN VACHON, APRIL 1940

"Atlanta, a natural way station of the hobo route in the South, gives thirty-day sentences in the city stockade or the chain gang . . . to anyone caught on a freight train in Fulton County," reported *Fortune* magazine. "Miami is friendly but firm. The city provides the wanderer with a bathing suit and the unescorted freedom of its famous beach. Afterwards, the vagrant is deported. Each day the so-called Hobo Express deposits eight or nine boys at the north line of the county with the warning that return will mean six months of [hard labor]."

Black youths had to contend with strict segregation laws in the South and with discrimination and racism wherever they went. Fifteen-year-old

Harold Jeffries and five friends rode the rails out of Minneapolis, Minnesota, in 1935. "As black kids from the North we'd heard of racial discrimination but not one of us had actual experience with harsh prejudice," he recalled. "Our first frightening encounter came at the Union Pacific roundhouse in Kansas City. Some of the kids drank from a 'Whites Only' fountain. We were literally run out of the [railroad] yards."

Some young whites in the segregated America of the 1930s had their first personal contact with blacks while riding the rails. Byron Bristol recalled a cold moonless night in 1933 when he was traveling from Kansas to Denver in a boxcar. At a stop in the dark, another rider climbed into the car. They struck up an animated conversation about their lives and families. "It was only at dawn that I discovered my traveling companion was black," Bristol said later. "It was surprising and enlightening for a boy who had been brought up in a white community."

In spite of hardships and dangers, many of the boxcar kids seemed to flourish. "It's two years since I left home," one boy told Minehan, "and I ain't never wanted to go back yet. . . . No, sir, the old road looks good to me. Square meals don't come every day, but I eat better than I ate at home and no grief about the old man being out of work all the time."

Robert Carter, a boxcar kid from Virginia, kept a diary of his wanderings through the South. "Arrived here on a freight train late at night, tired and dirty from train smoke and cinders," he wrote in Greenville, North Carolina. "I slept in the tobacco warehouse with two other young tramps,

A family traveling by freight train rests beside the tracks at Toppenish, Washington.
Photo by Dorothea Lange, August 1939

one having a suitcase crammed with dirty clothes and a blanket smelling of antiseptic. Next morning was cold, the wind hinted at winter. Leaving town I turned due south, walking the roads. All day I went steadily, getting an occasional ride from trucks or Fords. When dinnertime came I asked for work at a farmhouse for food and picked peas with the farmer's family for two hours. That night I pried open a church window and slept there."

On his arrival in Marion, Georgia, he wrote: "That night I slept in the Salvation Army. It was crowded with boys and young men, some with small grips, others with nothing but the shirts on their backs. One boy, a nightmare of rags and dirt, was so thin and far-gone that we tramps, ourselves destitute, gave him of our stock of goods."

People were sympathetic to the boxcar kids. Folks waved at them from the fields, from porches and backyards, as the freight went rattling past. When they got off the train, strangers invited them into their homes for a meal, pressed dollar bills into their hands on busy city street corners, offered them warm clothes, bought them bus tickets so they could ride back home in style. Years later, many of them looked back at their days on the road as the great adventure of their lives, a time when they were footloose, fearless, and free.

"My experience on the road gave me self-confidence," said another wanderer, René Champion. "I overcame a profound shyness and saw that I could shift for myself. I could survive and be respected by people. Without that experience, I don't know what kind of person I would've become."

Riding the rails near Bakersfield, California, April 1940.

THE LONE RANGER AND CAPTAIN MIDNIGHT

Checking out coming attractions at the Omar, West Virginia, movie house.

PHOTO BY BEN SHAHN, OCTOBER 1935

Kids who could afford to buy a ticket looked forward to Saturday afternoon at the movies. Admission to the Saturday matinee cost ten cents. That seemed like a lot of money during the Great Depression, but it bought a lot of entertainment.

For one thin dime a kid could see a double feature (two full-length movies), an animated cartoon, a short newsreel dealing with current events, a humorous short subject, and the latest episode of a serial—a continuing adventure story told one chapter a week. Along with all that, some theaters offered a bonus: a free ice cream or a frozen chocolate-covered banana.

The serial especially packed them in every Saturday. Each episode had a cliffhanger ending: The hero seemed hopelessly cornered by evildoers or

Lining up for the movie matinee in Pittsburgh, Pennsylvania.

PHOTO BY JACK DELANO,
JANUARY 1941

trapped by an avalanche, a stampede, a tidal wave, or some other catastrophe. Suspense built up all during the week as every movie fan tried to guess how the hero could possibly escape.

Favorite serial heroes included Tarzan of the Apes, Flash Gordon of the distant planet Mongo, and Wild West figures such as the Lone Ranger, who also appeared in many full-length features. These films were so involving that some kids brought cap guns to the theater and fired noisily at the outlaws and cattle rustlers on the silver screen. Theater owners began to insist that young gunslingers check their pistols at the movie-house door.

Along with the enormously popular westerns, children of the 1930s enjoyed certain movies that have been recognized as classics and are still being shown today. Walt Disney's *Snow White and the Seven Dwarfs* (1937) was the first full-length animated feature. It contained 250,000 individual drawings, broke all attendance records, and was translated into ten languages. Another perennial favorite, *The Wizard of Oz* (1939), begins as a black-and-white film. When Dorothy, played by sixteen-year-old Judy Garland, is swept up by a Kansas tornado to the magical land of Oz, the film's sudden switch to breathtaking color (at that time, a recent film innovation) always made audiences gasp.

Hollywood's top box-office star during the 1930s was a child, Shirley Temple. She made her first film in 1934, when she was five years old. By the time she was six, her films were taking in millions of dollars a year. She was often featured as an orphan who overcomes poverty and hardship through pluck and luck. Her rags-to-riches stories with their Hollywood-style happy endings helped Depression audiences forget hard times and escape, for an hour or two, to a world where everything was bound to turn out all right.

Kids who didn't have a dime for the movies could listen to the radio, the most popular form of home entertainment during the 1930s (commer-

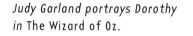

Judy Garland portrays Dorothy in The Wizard of Oz.

Child star Shirley Temple meets one of her fans, First Lady Eleanor Roosevelt, July 1938.

To Mrs. Roosevelt
Love,
Shirley Temple

cial television didn't arrive until the late 1940s). Back then, radio offered a much greater variety of programs than it does today. Hundreds of stations across the country broadcast soap operas, talent shows, serious dramas, comedy shows, mysteries, quizzes, sports events (especially baseball), and both classical and popular music programs.

Music was as important in the lives of young people then as it is now. The top bandleaders and vocalists of the era were as famous as movie stars.

Listening to the radio in Aberdeen, South Dakota.

Photo by John Vachon,
November 1940

Fans drew a sharp distinction between "sweet" bands, popularized by leaders such as Guy Lombardo, which featured a dreamy, sentimental (some said schmaltzy) sound, and "swing" bands, led by Benny Goodman, Glenn Miller, Duke Ellington, and others, with their driving rhythm and improvised solos akin to jazz. Teenagers clustered around their radios to listen to their favorite bands on weekly broadcasts. On Saturday evenings—before disc jockeys and Top 40 charts were commonplace—kids tuned in to *Your Hit Parade,* which presented the top ten tunes of the week, saving the top three hits for the end of the show.

SOME HIT TUNES OF THE 1930S

And the Angels Sing

A-Tisket A-Tasket

Deep Purple

Harbor Lights

Love Walked In

Moon over Miami

Over the Rainbow

Pennies from Heaven

Red Sails in the Sunset

The Way You Look Tonight

You Must Have Been a Beautiful Baby

Weekday evenings between five and six o'clock were known as "the children's hour" on radio. While dinner was being prepared, kids sat glued to the radio listening to a parade of suspenseful fifteen-minute radio serials, one after another. Many of these shows had kids as their main characters or as assistants to the adult hero. *Jack Armstrong, the All-American Boy* told the story of a brainy, brawny teenage athlete who plunged headlong into thrilling adventures all over the world with his friends Betty and Billy Fairfield, and their wise and witty Uncle Jim. Introduced in 1933 and broadcast regularly until 1951, this was one of the longest-running programs aimed at kids.

Westerns were as popular on the radio as they were on movie screens. *The Lone Ranger,* also introduced in 1933, was heard in at least twenty million homes, and the words "Hi-yo, Silver! Away!" shouted by the Lone Ranger as he mounted his Arabian stallion, Silver, were familiar to every kid in America. Parents liked the show because the Lone Ranger spoke perfect English and never shot to kill, although the outlaws he fought sometimes killed each other. He drew his pistols only in self-defense or to protect another's life, and when he did shoot, he fired silver bullets. He appeared in a radio serial, a movie serial, in feature-length films, in a 1950s television series, and in comic books.

Captain Midnight, another popular radio serial, followed the adventures of an undercover agent and airplane pilot who was constantly battling the evil plots of Ivan Shark and his nasty daughter, Fury. The captain was

Clayton Moore in character as the Lone Ranger. Moore was the best known of several actors who played the role on radio, in films, and on television.

aided in his efforts by his teenage friends Joyce and Chuck, who were members of his Secret Squadron. Young listeners could join the Secret Squadron by sending in a dime and the label from a jar of Ovaltine, one of the show's sponsors. In return, they received a special decoder badge, the Mystery Dial Code-O-Graph, which enabled them to decode the secret message broadcast at the end of each episode. *Captain Midnight,* which began in 1938, also moved to film and later to television.

The Aldrich Family, a weekly comedy show, centered on the adolescent mishaps of Henry Aldrich and appealed especially to teenagers. Henry was sixteen when the program began in 1939. He was still sixteen when it ended in 1953.

Radio shows had one big difference from television: Listeners had to use their imaginations in order to "see" the characters, the settings, and the action. "Mother would come to the door and holler, 'It's time for Jack Armstrong,'" one listener recalled. "And we would come in the living room. It was radio, so Jack Armstrong looked like whatever you wanted him to. You could imagine everything."

Imaginations were aided by the ingenious men and women who created radio sound effects. A wooden match snapped near the microphone sounded like a bat hitting a baseball. Horses galloping could be imitated by beating coconut shells on an old board. Twisting cellophane sounded like a crackling fire. Squeezing a box of cornstarch suggested footsteps in the snow. Sounds made manually on the spot were supplemented by recorded sounds—a speeding train, a barking dog, a roaring lion, a cheering crowd.

Most children growing up in the Great Depression didn't have a lot of money to spend on toys and games. Radio shows offered them a chance to obtain popular toys cheaply. Many of the shows were sponsored by cereal companies. By sending in cereal box tops and a coin or two—often a dime— kids could order kites, whistles, badges, tops, and hundreds of other wonderful treasures. The Hike-O-Meter, hooked to your belt, registered how many miles you hiked. The 5-Way-Detect-O-Scope was a cardboard-and-metal device for sighting objects and estimating their distance.

Jack Armstrong fans sent away for whistle rings like the one Jack wore. The ring arrived in the mail with a copy of Jack's secret whistle code. Other shows offered rings outfitted with secret compartments, with compasses, magnets, flashlights, and sirens, and with mirrors that allowed you to see behind you without turning your head. Some rings glowed in the dark. Because the rings were made of cheap metal, most of them turned the wearer's finger green after a few days.

Some families could not afford to buy the packaged breakfast cereals and other products that sponsored radio shows. When it came to box tops and the toys and gadgets you could get with them, many poor kids were out of luck. But they could always make their own toys. One of the most popular homemade toys during the 1930s was the rubber-band gun, made from a piece of wood, a clothespin, and a rubber band. Kids pretending to be cowboys or detectives could shoot a rubber band ten feet or more with one of

these. With a crayon or a bit of paint, wooden clothespins could also be transformed into dolls, soldiers, and other make-believe people.

Two tin cans, connected by a long string, served as a kind of primitive walkie-talkie. By speaking into one can, you could communicate with a distant friend who was holding the open end of the other can against one ear.

Boys held racing contests with homemade "push-mobiles" or "sidewalk racers." All that was needed to build one was a discarded milk box or crate from the grocery store, a long wooden plank from a construction site, and a pair of old clamp-on steel roller skates. (Rollerblades and skateboards were in the distant future.) A kid would nail the skates to either end of the plank as wheels. The crate was nailed to the top of the plank, up front. Tin cans might be added as "headlights" or "tail-lights," along with an old license plate or automobile hood ornament. Standing on the wooden plank with one foot, and holding on to the sides of the crate, a boy would power his racer with

Playing jacks, Pinal County, Arizona, April 1940.

Playing marbles, South Side of Chicago, April 1941. Jacks and marbles were popular games that could be played anywhere without spending much money.

PHOTOS BY RUSSELL LEE

his free foot and a helping push at the top of a steep hill. These simple Depression-era racers, built with scavenged materials, developed into the Soapbox Derby competitions held nationally today.

Several million families were too poor during the Great Depression even to own a radio. Out of nearly thirty-four million American households in 1938, about twenty-seven million, or 79 percent, possessed radios. Today, 98.2 percent of American households have at least one TV set.

Playing an old phonograph in a sharecropper's home in Transylvania, Louisiana.
PHOTO BY RUSSELL LEE

Watching a puppet show,
Red House, West Virginia.

Photo by Ben Shahn, 1937

Kids who could not tune in to the popular shows of the 1930s often felt isolated and lonely. "We are just poor renters on a farm and there is no money for a radio or the books I like so much," a fourteen-year-old Texas girl wrote to Eleanor Roosevelt. "Dear First Lady, I have read of your kind heartedness and the cheer you have brought to so many. Can't you suggest some way that I can get a radio so I can hear the music and talk and news from outside my very small little world?"

A BRIGHTER TOMORROW

In 1939—ten years after the stock market collapsed—two spectacular year-long world's fairs offered Americans a generous helping of optimism and hope.

San Francisco's Golden Gate International Exposition opened on February 18 on a four-hundred-acre landfill in San Francisco Bay called Treasure Island, the world's largest man-made island. The fair celebrated the completion of two impressive engineering feats: the Oakland–San Francisco Bay Bridge and the Golden Gate Bridge, which spanned the entrance to San Francisco Bay. And it featured some eye-popping technological exhibits, among them a robot named Willie Vocalite and a keyboard-operated talking machine called Pedro the Vodor.

Treasure Island, site of San Francisco's Golden Gate International Exposition, 1939.

The New York World's Fair opened on April 30 on a twelve-hundred-acre site just five miles from downtown Manhattan, in the borough of Queens. The theme of that fair was "The World of Tomorrow," and it featured its own array of futuristic exhibits, including a robot named Elektro, a simulated trip to the moon, and the first public demonstration of television.

Both fairs promised a brighter tomorrow, suggesting that American ingenuity would always triumph over hard times. And yet in 1939, the Great Depression, while not as severe as it had been a few years earlier, had still not been defeated.

Jamming every inch of space in the huge Hall of Electrical Living at the New York World's Fair, a rapt crowd watches the robot Elektro perform his twenty-six mechanical tricks, including walking, talking, and counting on his fingers.

Another futuristic marvel—television—attracts a curious crowd at the New York World's Fair RCA exhibit.

When President Roosevelt took office six years earlier, on March 4, 1933, the nation's economy seemed perilously close to a complete breakdown. Critics had complained that Herbert Hoover, the president at the outbreak of the Depression, hadn't done enough to rescue the economy and help those who were suffering. Roosevelt promised "action and action now." He pledged "a new deal for the American people," and he moved swiftly. The term "New Deal" became the watchword of his administration.

New Deal programs provided relief for the needy, created hundreds of thousands of jobs for the unemployed, and introduced social and economic reforms that have become a lasting part of American life. Some of those reforms, enacted during the 1930s and still in place today, were designed to prevent another economic catastrophe.

Schoolgirls of the Great Depression, Red House, West Virginia.
PHOTO BY BEN SHAHN, 1935

Federal bank insurance guarantees that Americans will never again lose their life's savings because of a bank failure; each bank deposit is now insured by the government for up to $100,000. Unemployment compensation and Social Security provide a safety net to help prevent the great human suffering of the 1930s from happening again. And laws regulating the financial markets and protecting investors have helped soften the impact of economic downturns since World War II. As a result, those downturns, or recessions, have been much milder and have caused much less distress than the Great Depression.

Roosevelt was a controversial president who excited strong feelings. His opponents charged that he was strangling the free enterprise system and turning the country into a welfare state. But he was also criticized for being

Schoolboys of the Great Depression, Red House, West Virgina.

Children of a Dust Bowl refugee at a migrant camp in California.
PHOTO BY DOROTHEA LANGE, NOVEMBER 1936

too timid, for not doing enough to change the economic system that had caused so much misery. His admirers said that his policies eased the worst suffering of the Great Depression, rescued the economy, and gave people hope.

"Those suffering hardship from no fault of their own have a right to call upon the Government for aid," Roosevelt told Congress in 1938, "and a government worthy of its name must make a fitting response." For the first time in the nation's history, the federal government had made itself responsible for those citizens who had been victimized by economic forces beyond their control.

Despite the New Deal's accomplishments, the Depression stubbornly resisted efforts to restore prosperity. Unemployment persisted through the

1930s. It took a different kind of crisis, the outbreak of World War II, to put every employable man and woman back to work in the nation's booming defense industries. Massive government spending for the war effort finally brought an end to the longest and worst economic depression America had ever known.

Hitler's bombs were falling on London when the world's fairs in New York and San Francisco closed in 1940. A year later, following the Japanese attack on Pearl Harbor on December 7, 1941, the United States entered World War II, and the young people who were children during the Great Depression were called on to face another national crisis. They fought in Europe and the Pacific, and when they came home, eager to get on with their lives and optimistic about the future, they helped build the strongest economy the United States had ever known.

They became the parents of the baby boomer generation—those born in the two decades after the war ended in 1945—and the grandparents and great-grandparents of children growing up today. They prospered as no Americans before them ever had. But they never forgot what it had meant to be young and needy during America's Great Depression.

"There were times when we didn't know whether we'd have anything to eat at night," remembered Robert Baird, who grew up in Depression-era Detroit and later became a successful businessman in the Pacific Northwest. "I tell that to my children today, and they think the old man's flipped his lid."

CHAPTER NOTES

The following notes indicate the sources of quoted material included in the text. Each citation indicates the first and last words or phrases of the quotation and its source. Unless otherwise noted, references are to works cited in the Selected Bibliography beginning on page 109. All Meltzer citations refer to his *Brother, Can You Spare a Dime?*

CHAPTER 1: "THE SIGHT OF MY FATHER CRYING"

Page

3   "We had owned . . . coal bin": Jellison, p. 14

4   "My mother cries . . . help out": Cohen, p. 21

5   "We saw the city . . . like animals": Watkins, *Hungry Years*, p. 57

8   "Did the thought . . . we were making?": Watkins, *Hungry Years*, p. 48

9   "I knew . . . home": Terkel, p. 89

11   Depression Shopping List, adapted from Britten and Brash, p. 29

11   Average Annual Earnings, adapted from Britten and Brash, p. 26

Daughter of a cotton sharecropper, Hale County, Alabama.

PHOTO BY WALKER EVANS, ABOUT 1935

CHAPTER 2: "ILL-HOUSED, ILL-CLAD, ILL-NOURISHED"

Page

13   "The first hard times . . . over that": Meltzer, p. 27

13   "In this nation . . . ill-nourished": from FDR's second inaugural address, January 20, 1937

14   "We owe . . . don't have shoes": Ira Peck, Steven Jantzen, and Daniel Rosen, *American Adventures* (New York: Scholastic Book Services, 1979), p. 480

15   "For a whole week . . . I guess": Meltzer, p. 27

17   "We have lived . . . come true": Cohen, p. 82

17   "I solemnly . . . 2 yrs": Cohen, p. 54

17   "it just makes . . . dress decent": Cohen, p. 23

17   "my poor mother . . . to us": Cohen, p. 151

17   "Though we are poor . . . admit it": Cohen, p. 16

19   "We ain't . . . moving again": Watkins, *Hungry Years*, p. 57

19   "My father . . . sensitive": Cohen, p. 19

23   "Along the Hudson . . . dispossessed": Bendiner, p. 4

23   "Grandma . . . stop and think": Thompson and Austin, unpaged

23   "With no dependable . . . Christmas": Hastings, pp. 13–15

27   "I was a sophomore . . . the car": Jellison, p. 9

CHAPTER 3: IN AND OUT OF SCHOOL

Page

29   "Because of . . . management" and "I changed . . . rooming house": Parks, pp. 54–55

32   "With the school closed . . . set of books?": Uys, p. 22

32   "In a moment . . . school teachers": Meltzer, p. 30

35   "Whenever you have . . . nothing at all": Watkins, *Hungry Years*, p. 62

35   "I can't . . . turn to eat": Watkins, *Hungry Years*, p. 62

35   "for the first time" and "Not once . . . to the radio": Levine, pp. 37–38

37   "I find . . . leave home in": Cohen, p. 93

39   "My folks . . . hard to make it": Cohen, p. 110

CHAPTER 4: KIDS AT WORK

Page

41   "There are no . . . early": Lumpkin and Douglas, p. 145

41   "It's better . . . for their living": Lumpkin and Douglas, p. 146

42   "I don't expect . . . back to school": Thompson and Austin, unpaged

42   "If our eyes . . . be found": Lumpkin and Douglas, p. 15

43   "At 5:30 . . . hoping for work": Lumpkin and Douglas, p. 13

44   "because I wanted . . . burden to them": Cohen, p. 140

44   "If I wasn't . . . rear table": Kisseloff, p. 361

48   "Maybe you . . . come home": Watkins, *Hungry Years*, p. 268

49   "I have moments . . . the community": Cohen, p. 13

51   "Words cannot . . . thousands of others": Cohen, p. 10

51   "It was . . . this world": Elder, p. 64

CHAPTER 5: "OKIE, GO HOME!"

Page

53   "I have to get up . . . I am late": Cohen, p. 181

53   "I have done . . . world is": Cohen, p. 15

54   "It was . . . an event": Terkel, p. 96

54   "If they come . . . my cattle": Meltzer, p. 87

56   "old enough to 'make hands'": Lumpkin and Douglas, p. 4

56   "Tom gets up . . . in one pair": Lumpkin and Douglas, pp. 5–6

60 "The impact . . . possessions": quoted in Winslow, p. 89

60 "If you . . . ever seen": quoted in Watkins, *Great Depression*, p. 188

61 "The land . . . go somewhere": Winslow, p. 91

64 "The typical . . . appalling": quoted in Winslow, p. 96

65 "dozens of children . . . sore throats": Watkins, *Great Depression*, p. 202

67 "shiftless trash . . . dogs": Stanley, p. 34

67 "vile propaganda": Stanley, p. 43

CHAPTER 6: BOXCAR KIDS

Page

71 "It was . . . knows where": Uys, p. 57

72 "the vast homeless horde": quoted in Watkins, *Hungry Years*, p. 70

74 "Mobs of men . . . on an outing": Minehan, p. xiii

74 "In boxcars . . . is absent": Minehan, p. 61

74 "It was easier . . . for a boy": Uys, p. 97

74 "Why did you . . . from home": Minehan, p. 48

75 "It was dangerous . . . to survive": Uys, p. 133

77 "Atlanta . . . [hard labor]": quoted in Meltzer, p. 33

79 "As black kids . . . yards": Uys, p. 113

79 "It was only . . . white community": Uys, p. 115

79 "It's two . . . all the time": Minehan, p. 43

79 "Arrived here . . . slept there": quoted in Meltzer, p. 33

81 "That night . . . stock of goods": Meltzer, p. 34

81 "My experience . . . would've become": Uys, p. 129

CHAPTER 7: *THE LONE RANGER* AND *CAPTAIN MIDNIGHT*

Page

87   Some Hit Tunes of the 1930s, adapted from Britten and Brash, p. 140

89   "Mother would . . . imagine everything": Thompson and Austin, unpaged

93   "We are just . . . small little world?": Cohen, p. 182

CHAPTER 8: A BRIGHTER TOMORROW

Page

100   "Those suffering . . . fitting response": quoted in William E. Leuchtenburg, "Why the Candidates Still Use FDR as Their Measure," *American Heritage,* Feb. 1988, p. 40

101   "There were times . . . flipped his lid": Terkel, p. 341

SELECTED BIBLIOGRAPHY

Surprisingly, few scholarly works have examined the impact of the Great Depression on children and teens who grew up during those perilous years. The only book-length study was written by a sociologist, Glen H. Elder, Jr., whose *Children of the Great Depression*: *Social Change in Life Experience* (Boulder, Colo.: Westview Press, 1999; originally published by the University of Chicago Press in 1974) is recognized as a pioneering contribution to theory and method in the study of lives. Based on extensive interviews of 167 individuals born in 1920–1921, whom Elder followed from their elementary-school days in Oakland, California, through the 1960s, the study assesses the influence on these individuals of the economic crisis and, in the expanded 1999 edition, of World War II and the Korean War. This is a seminal work, replete with charts, graphs, and statistics, rather than an anecdotal account for the general reader.

Among many informative histories of the Depression era, I found the following especially helpful: T. H. Watkins's *The Hungry Years: A Narrative History of the Great Depression in America* (New York: Henry Holt, 1999) along with his *The Great*

Depression: America in the 1930s (Boston: Little, Brown, 1993); David M. Kennedy's Pulitzer Prize–winning *Freedom from Fear: The American People in Depression and War, 1929–1945* (New York: Oxford University Press, 1999); Robert S. McElvaine's *The Great Depression: America, 1929–l941* (2nd ed.: New York: Times Books, 1993); and Milton Meltzer's *Brother, Can You Spare a Dime? The Great Depression, 1929–1933* (New York: Facts on File, 199l; originally published in a different form by Alfred A. Knopf in 1969).

I also consulted and enjoyed Robert Bendiner's *Just Around the Corner: A Highly Selective History of the Thirties* (New York: Harper and Row, 1967); Don Congdon, ed., *The Thirties: A Time to Remember* (New York: Simon & Schuster, 1962); Charles A. Jellison's *Tomatoes Were Cheaper: Tales from the Thirties* (Syracuse, N.Y.: Syracuse University Press, 1977); and Richard Lowitt and Maurine Beasley, eds., *One Third of a Nation: Lorena Hickock Reports on the Great Depression* (Urbana, Ill.: University of Illinois Press, 1981).

Memoirs offered a more personal point of view, among them: Robert J. Hastings's *A Nickel's Worth of Skim Milk: A Boy's View of the Great Depression* (Carbondale, Ill.: Southern Illinois University Graphics and Publications, 1972); Philip Levine's *The Bread of Time: Toward an Autobiography* (New York: Alfred A. Knopf, 1994); and Gordon Parks's *A Choice of Weapons* (St. Paul, Minn.: Minnesota Historical Society Press, 1986).

Studs Terkel's *Hard Times: An Oral History of the Great Depression* (New York: Pantheon Books, 1970) is the definitive oral history of the period. I also drew from Jeff Kisseloff's *You Must Remember This: An Oral History of Manhattan from the 1890s to World War II* (Baltimore: Johns Hopkins University Press, 1999).

The letters written by children to Eleanor Roosevelt are from Robert Cohen, ed., *Dear Mrs. Roosevelt: Letters from Children of the Great Depression* (Chapel Hill, N.C.: University of North Carolina Press, 2002), a collection that also provides valuable background information.

My chapter on child labor during the Depression was informed by Katharine DuPre Lumpkin and Dorothy Wolff Douglas's contemporary account, *Child Workers in America*

(New York: Robert M. McBride, 1937). And my chapter on boxcar kids drew on another contemporary account, Thomas Minehan's *Boy and Girl Tramps of America* (New York: Farrar and Rinehart, 1934). A recent book about boxcar kids of the 1930s, based on more than 500 interviews and the subject of a documentary film, is Errol Lincoln Uys's *Riding the Rails: Teenagers on the Move During the Great Depression* (New York: Routledge, 2003).

My discussion of migrant farm workers is based in part on James Noble Gregory's *American Exodus: The Dust Bowl Migration and Okie Culture in California* (New York: Oxford University Press, 1989); Donald E. Worster's *Dust Bowl: The Southern Plains in the 1930s* (New York: Oxford University Press, 1979); and Tricia Andryszewski's *The Dust Bowl: Disaster on the Plains* (Brookfield, Conn.: The Millbrook Press, 1993).

For books on the popular culture of the period, see Gary Dean Best's *The Nickel and Dime Decade: American Popular Culture During the 1930s* (Westport, Conn.: Praeger, 1993); and J. Fred MacDonald's *Don't Touch That Dial! Radio Programming in American Life, 1920–1960* (Chicago: Nelson-Hall, 1979).

Among numerous photo essays and photo albums, I consulted Kathleen Thompson and Hilary Mac Austin, eds., *Children of the Depression* (Bloomington, Ind.: Indiana University Press, 2001); Loretta Britten and Sarah Brash, eds., *Hard Times: The 30s* (New York: Time-Life Books, 1998); Susan Winslow's *Brother, Can You Spare a Dime? America from the Wall Street Crash to Pearl Harbor: An Illustrated Documentary* (New York: Paddington Press, 1979); and James D. Horan's *The Desperate Years: A Pictorial History of the Thirties* (New York: Bonanza Books, 1962).

Books for young readers include Karen Blumenthal's *Six Days in October: The Stock Market Crash of 1929* (New York: Simon & Schuster/Atheneum, 2002); Michael L. Cooper's *Dust to Eat: Drought and Depression in the 1930s* (New York: Clarion Books, 2004); my book *Franklin Delano Roosevelt* (New York: Clarion Books, 1990); Milton Meltzer's *Driven from the Land: The Story of the Dust Bowl* (Tarrytown, N.Y.: Benchmark Books, 2000) and his *Brother, Can You Spare a Dime?*, mentioned on page 66; Anne E. Schraff's *The Great Depression and the New Deal: America's Economic Collapse and Recovery* (New York: Franklin Watts, 1990); and Jerry Stanley's *Children of the Dust Bowl: The True Story of the School at Weedpatch Camp* (New York: Crown, 1992).

The New Deal Network, an educational guide to the Great Depression with links to documents, photos, art, etc., is at http://newdeal.feri.org. Images from the Farm Security Administration collection are available online by typing in "Library of Congress Prints and Photographs" on any Internet search engine.

PICTURE SOURCES

All photographs not specifically credited below are from the Farm Security Administration collection, Prints and Photographs Division, Library of Congress. All are hereby gratefully acknowledged.

AP/Wide World Photos: 7, 20–21, 60 (left), 85 (left), 88, 97 (top)

Franklin D. Roosevelt Library: 14, 38, 49, 50, 60 (center), 85 (right)

National Archives: 70, 73, 76, 80

INDEX

Note: Page numbers in **bold** type refer to illustrations.